STEP-BY-STEP™
DRAW
TANKS

MARK BERGIN

BOOK HOUSE

This edition first published in MMXVII by
Book House

Distributed by Black Rabbit Books
P.O. Box 3263
Mankato
Minnesota MN 56002

Cataloging-in-Publication Data is available
from the Library of Congress

Printed in the United States
At Corporate Graphics,
North Mankato, Minnesota

9 8 7 6 5 4 3 2 1

ISBN: 978-1-911242-24-6

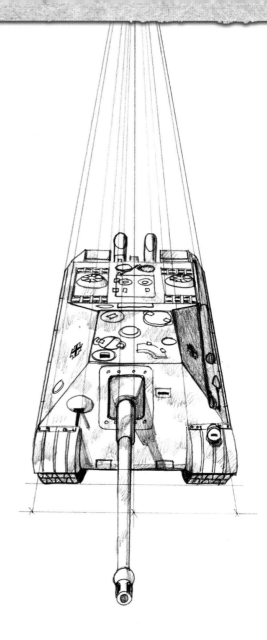

CONTENTS

MAKING A START

Learning to draw is about looking and seeing. Keep practicing and get to know your subject. Start by doodling, and experiment with shapes and patterns. There are many ways to draw; this book cannot show all of them. Visit art galleries, look at artists' drawings, see how friends draw, but above all, find your own way.

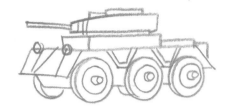

Use a sketchbook to make quick drawings like these.

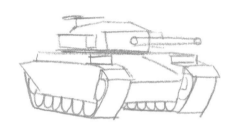

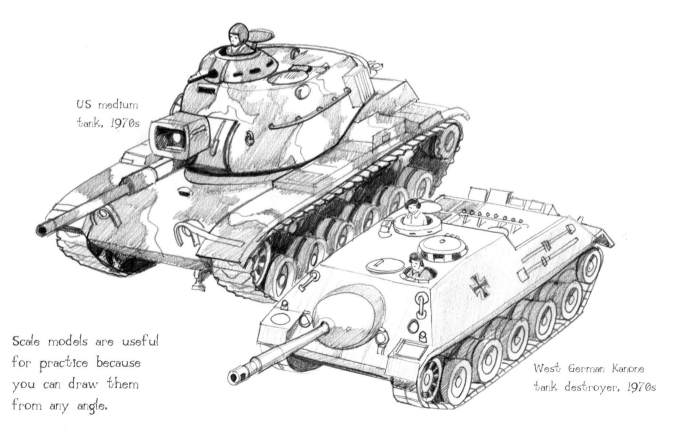

US medium tank, 1970s

Scale models are useful for practice because you can draw them from any angle.

West German Kanone tank destroyer, 1970s

German Tiger 1 tank

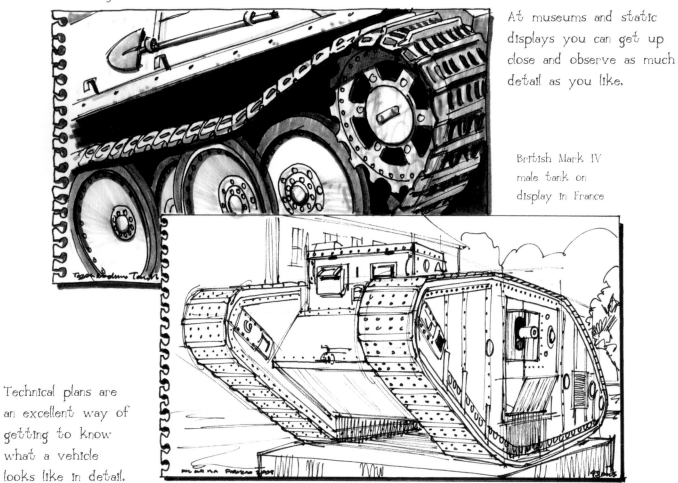

At museums and static displays you can get up close and observe as much detail as you like.

British Mark IV male tank on display in France

Technical plans are an excellent way of getting to know what a vehicle looks like in detail.

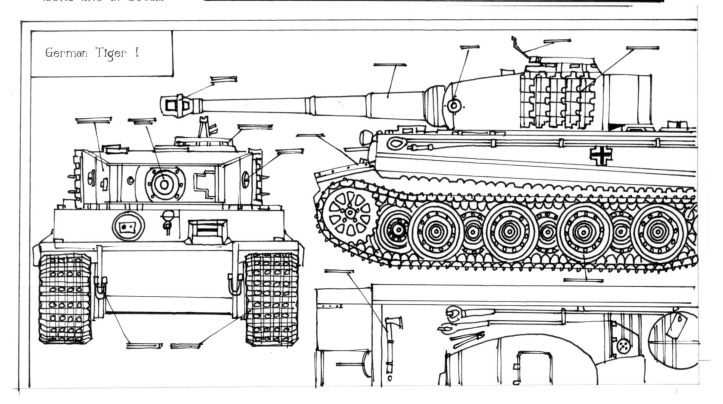

German Tiger 1

BASIC CONSTRUCTION

Use simple shapes such as circles, rectangles, and squares to sketch the basic construction of the vehicle. Get the proportions and perspective right before you start adding more detail.

Ignore distracting details and concentrate on getting the overall shape right.

Try tilting the vehicle to make it look as though it is going uphill or downhill. It may help to draw the ground surface first.

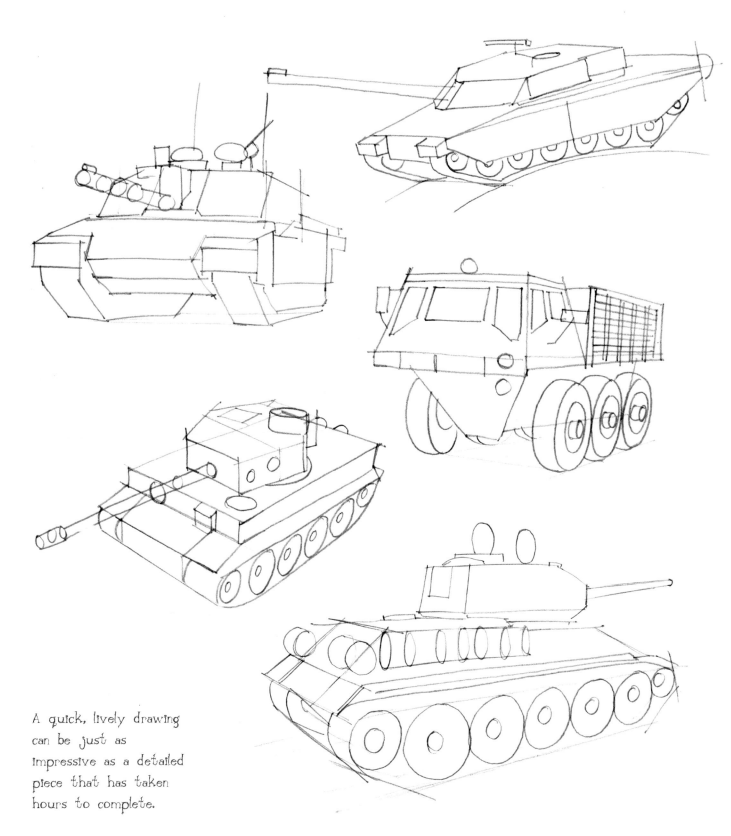

A quick, lively drawing can be just as impressive as a detailed piece that has taken hours to complete.

STYLE AND MEDIUM

Try using different types of drawing paper and materials to create different results. Experiment with charcoal, wax crayons, and pastels, or use dark ink to make a striking silhouette.

Silhouette is a style of drawing that uses only a solid black shape, like a shadow.

German Panzer 38(t):
ink silhouette

Soft **pastels** might seem too delicate to use for military vehicles, but they are perfect for smudging together to make a muddy or smoky background. White pastel can be added to give highlights on metallic surfaces. Ask an adult to coat the finished drawing with fixative to prevent further smudging.

Felt-tips come in a range of widths. Use the wide ones for large areas of shade and the finer ones for details.

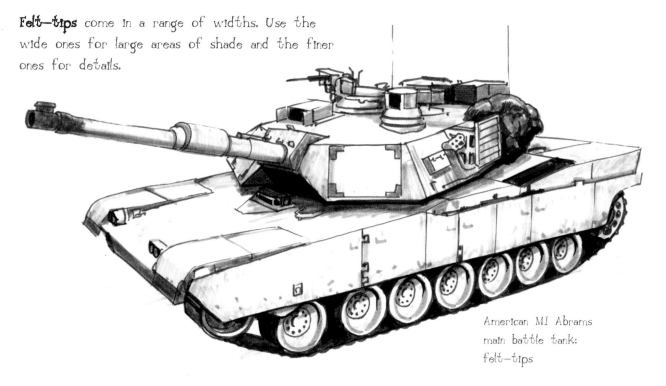

American M1 Abrams
main battle tank:
felt-tips

British Churchill
tank: pencil

Hard **pencils** are grayer and soft pencils are blacker. Hard pencils are usually graded from 6H (the hardest) through 5H, 4H, 3H, and 2H to H. Soft pencils are graded from B, 2B, 3B, 4B, and 5B up to 6B (the softest). HB, the commonest grade, comes between H and B.

Lines drawn in **ink** cannot be erased, so keep your ink drawings sketchy and less rigid. Don't worry about mistakes, as these lines can be lost in the drawing as it develops.

German Tiger I tank: ink pen

PERSPECTIVE

If you look at any object from different viewpoints, you will see that the parts that are closest to you look larger, and the parts farther away look smaller. Perspective uses this effect to make the drawing look three-dimensional, even though the paper surface is flat.

The **vanishing point (V.P.)** is where the parallel construction lines appear to meet. A low V.P. (below) makes the tank loom up as if you are looking up at it from below. A high V.P. (right) gives the impression that you are looking down at the vehicle.

The construction lines become closer together as they approach the V.P., so the back of the tank (the end farthest away) appears narrower than the front.

Use construction lines to keep all the parts of the tank in proportion.

V.P. = vanishing point

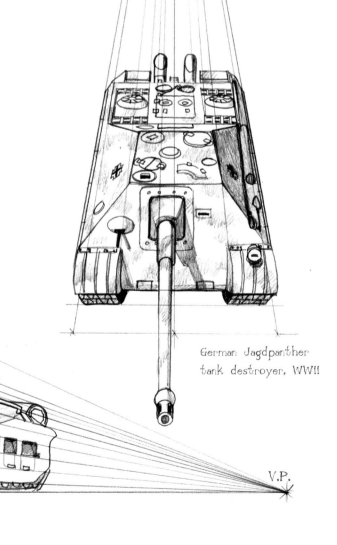

German Jagdpanther tank destroyer, WWII

British Matilda II, WWII

Two-point perspective uses two V.P.s: one for lines running along the length of the object, and another for lines running across its width.

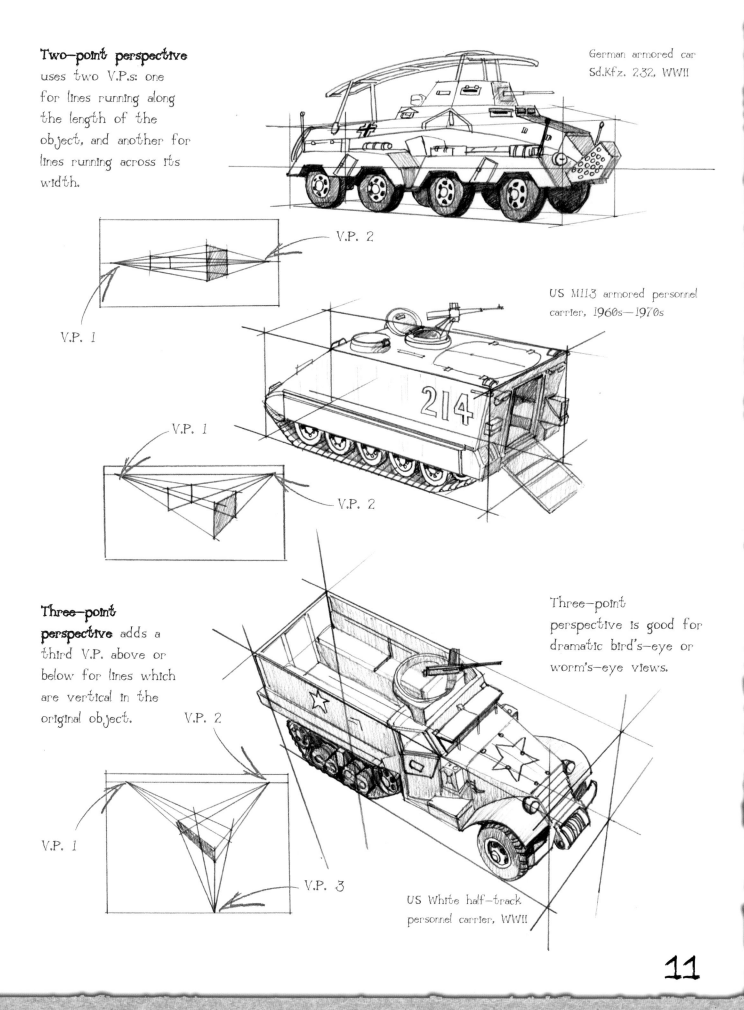

German armored car Sd.Kfz. 232, WWII

V.P. 2

V.P. 1

V.P. 1

V.P. 2

US M113 armored personnel carrier, 1960s—1970s

Three-point perspective adds a third V.P. above or below for lines which are vertical in the original object.

Three-point perspective is good for dramatic bird's-eye or worm's-eye views.

V.P. 2

V.P. 1

V.P. 3

US White half-track personnel carrier, WWII

11

USING PHOTOS

Drawing from photographs is particularly useful if you don't have access to the original object.

Russian T-34-85 tank, WWII

Find a good photograph of your chosen tank and trace it.

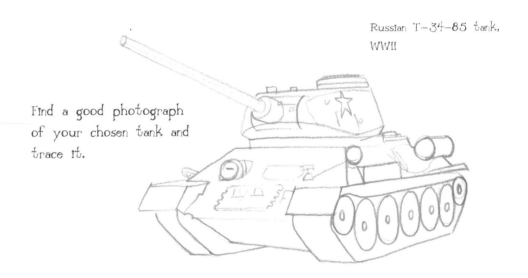

Using a ruler, mark out a grid of equal-sized squares over your traced drawing.

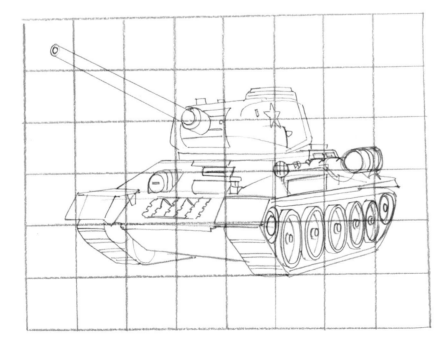

Decide which direction the light is coming from in your picture, and put in areas of shadow where the light doesn't reach.

Light source

Eye level

Faintly draw a grid with the same number of squares on your drawing paper. You can enlarge or reduce your drawing by changing the size of the squares.

Now copy the shapes from each square of the tracing paper onto your drawing paper.

The eye level in this drawing is that of a person standing up. If your tank is on a level surface, the left and right vanishing points are on the viewer's eye level.

Now you can add final details, and a background if you wish.

MARK IV TANK

The British Mark IV tank was first used in 1917. The one shown here is a "male" tank, with 6-pounder guns; "female" tanks had only machine guns.

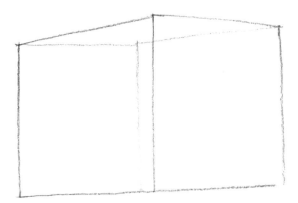

Start by sketching a simple box in perspective.

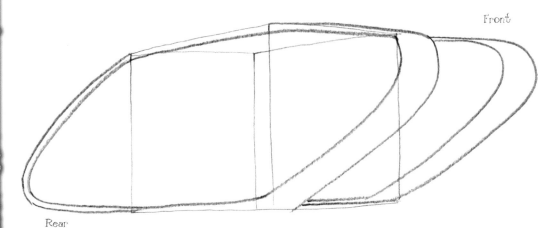

Front

Rear

Use sweeping, curved lines to create the shape of the caterpillar tracks at front and rear.

The driver's cab is another simple box drawn in perspective. Add small rectangles for the vision ports.

Cab

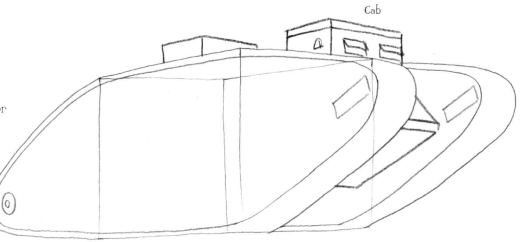

Draw the sponson: this is the armored box on the side of the tank that holds the 6-pounder gun.

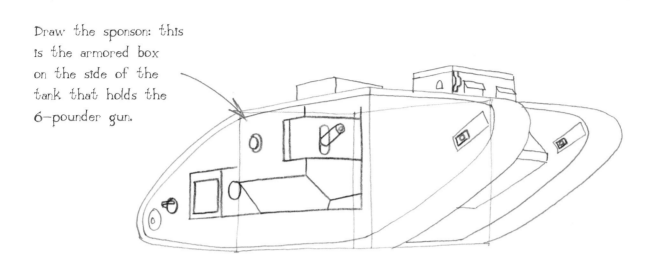

Use short, evenly spaced lines to show the ridges on the caterpillar tracks.

Add details to the hull, such as the radiator grille towards the rear.

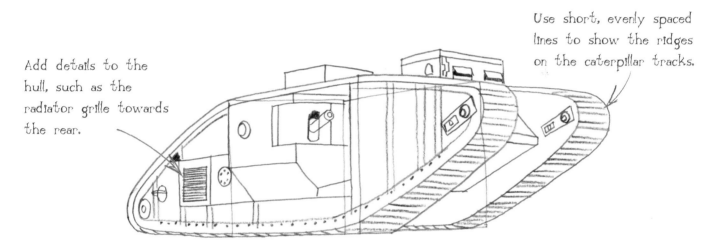

Draw deep shadows on the parts that face away from the light.

Add as much detail as you like. It's up to you whether you include the rivets.

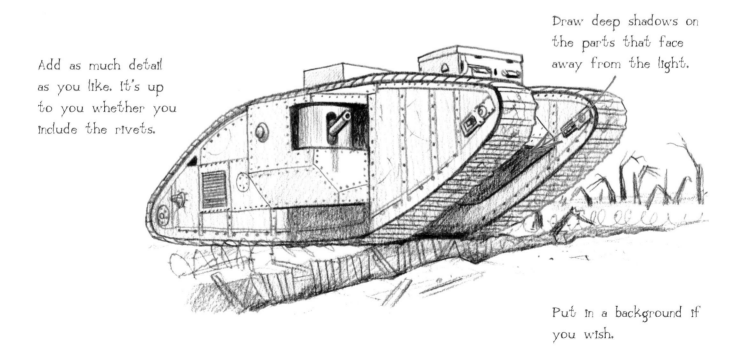

Put in a background if you wish.

15

HALF-TRACK

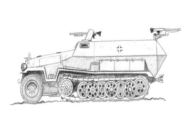

Half-tracks have ordinary wheels at the front and tracks at the back. This makes them much easier to steer than a tank. This is the German Hanomag Sd.Kfz. 251 of 1939.

Draw a rectangle for the main body of the vehicle, and a wedge shape for the hood.

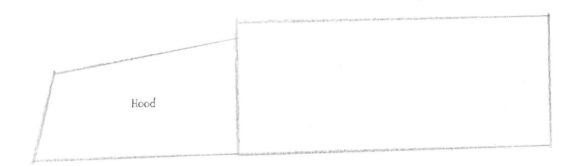

Hood

The edges of the armor plating are formed entirely from straight lines. Pay attention to the angles.

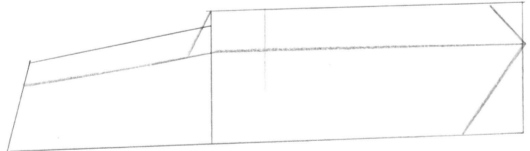

Sketch in the headlights and vision slits. The wheel arch runs the whole length of the vehicle.

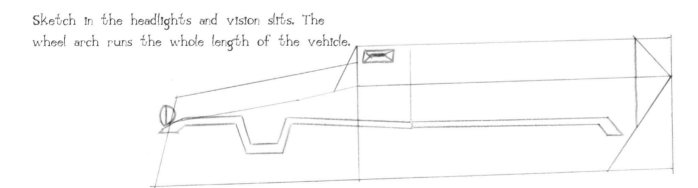

Draw the wheels. Note how some of them overlap.

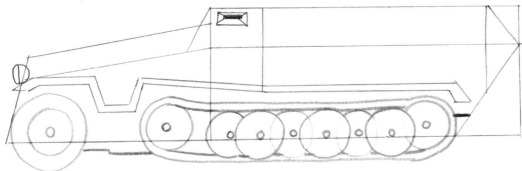

This model is mounted with anti-tank and anti-aircraft guns.

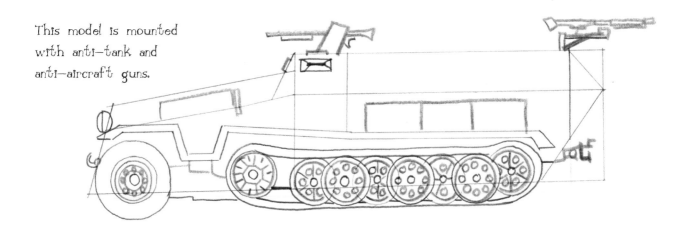

Remember to think about where the light source is and how this affects the shadows in your drawing.

The top of the bodywork is angled upward and catches the light: use little tone.

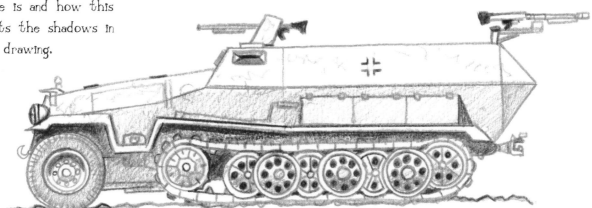

Very little light reaches under the wheel arches: use heavy tone.

SHERMAN TANK

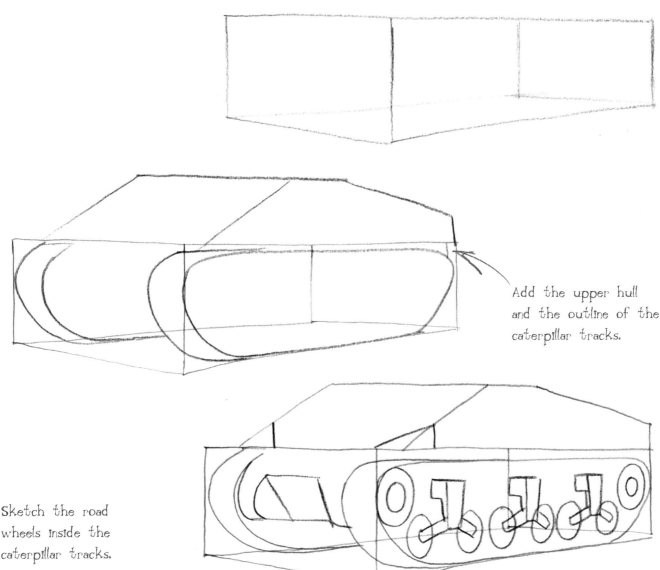

The M4 Sherman tank was designed in the USA and used throughout the Second World War. It was not heavily armored, but was lighter and faster than other tanks.

Draw a rectangular box in perspective.

Add the upper hull and the outline of the caterpillar tracks.

Sketch the road wheels inside the caterpillar tracks.

Add the turret and the gun.

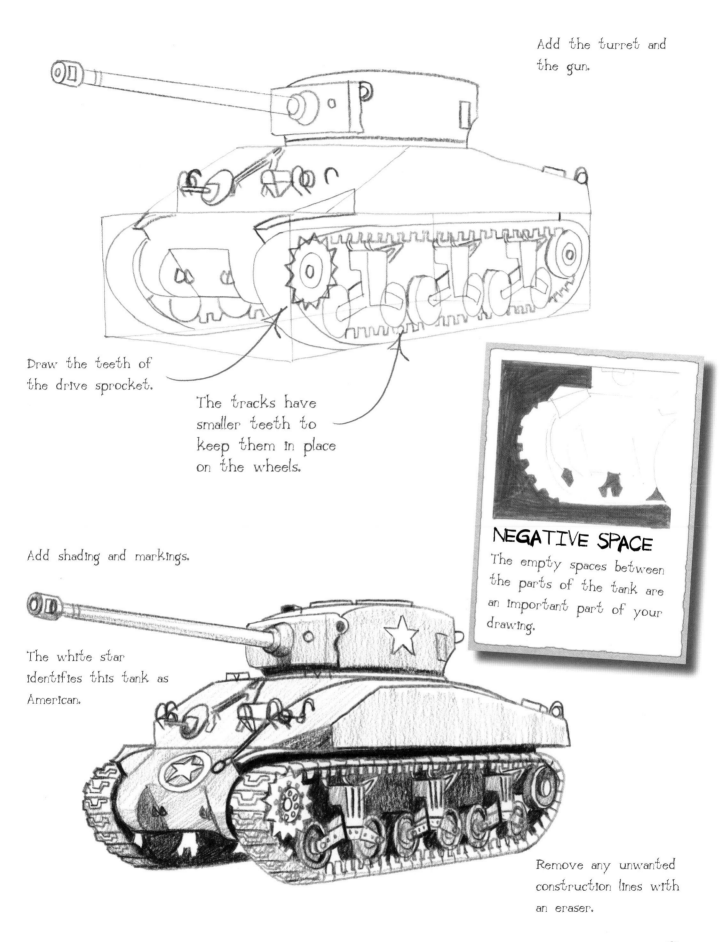

Draw the teeth of the drive sprocket.

The tracks have smaller teeth to keep them in place on the wheels.

Add shading and markings.

The white star identifies this tank as American.

NEGATIVE SPACE
The empty spaces between the parts of the tank are an important part of your drawing.

Remove any unwanted construction lines with an eraser.

PANZER IV

The German Panzer IV was in use throughout the Second World War. It was deployed for both infantry-support and anti-tank combat. Many versions were made; this is type D.

Draw a rectangular box in perspective. This will be the upper part of the tank's hull.

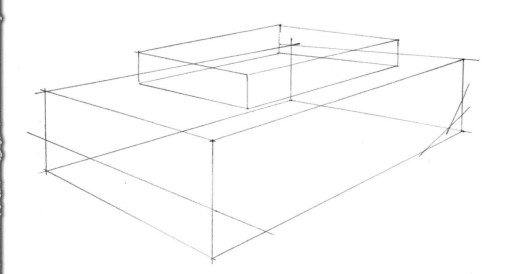

Add a larger box to represent the shape of the lower hull, wheels and tracks.

Shape and detail the front of the hull, using straight lines.

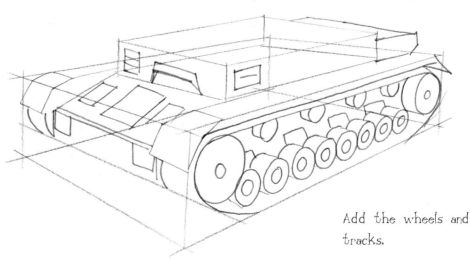

Add the wheels and tracks.

The turret is quite a complex shape. The hatches are shown open so that the machine gun can be used.

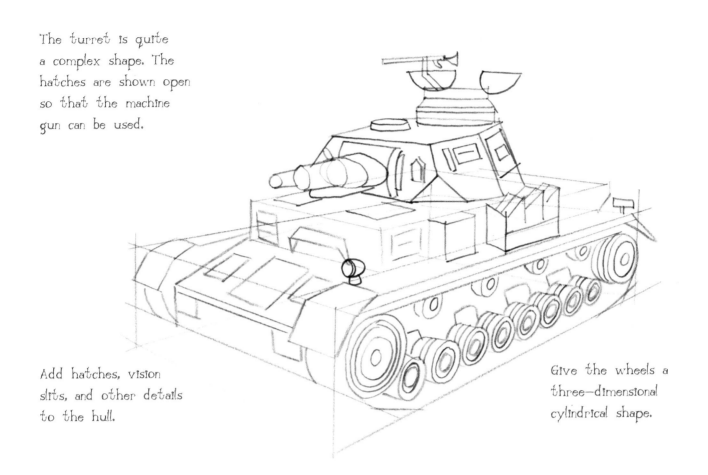

Add hatches, vision slits, and other details to the hull.

Give the wheels a three-dimensional cylindrical shape.

Think about which direction the light is coming from, and use shading for areas that the light doesn't reach. This makes the drawing look three-dimensional.

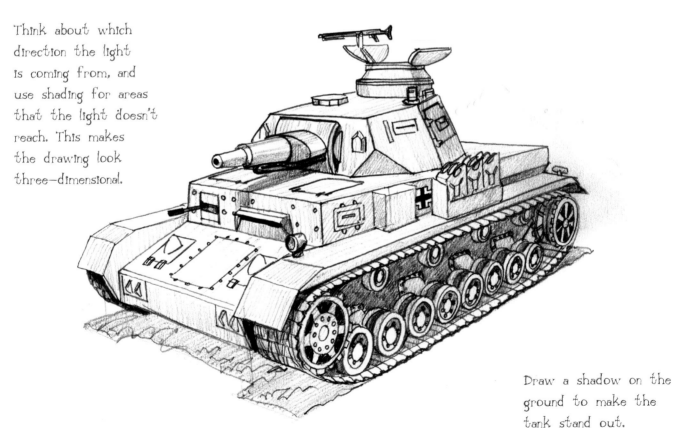

Draw a shadow on the ground to make the tank stand out.

TIGER I TANK

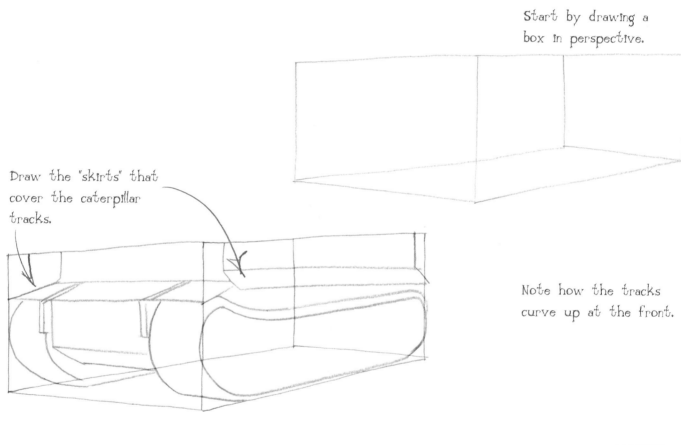

The German Tiger I was designed by Dr Ferdinand Porsche in 1942. This heavily armed tank fought on all fronts, from Russia to North Africa.

Start by drawing a box in perspective.

Draw the "skirts" that cover the caterpillar tracks.

Note how the tracks curve up at the front.

Add the road wheels; note how they overlap for protection.

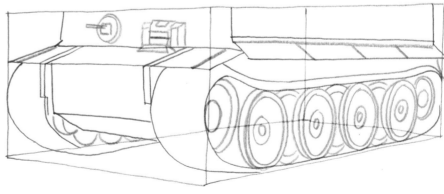

Draw the Tiger's
turret and powerful
88 mm gun.

Add as much detail
as you wish, such as
vision ports, and the
bolts where the gun
joins the turret.

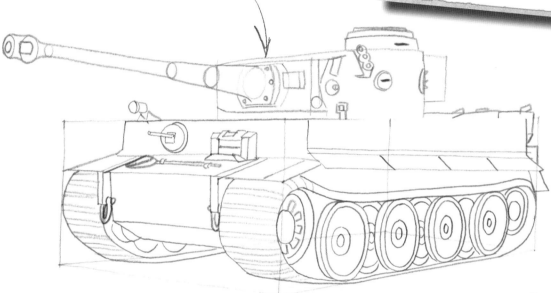

Remove any unwanted
construction lines with
an eraser.

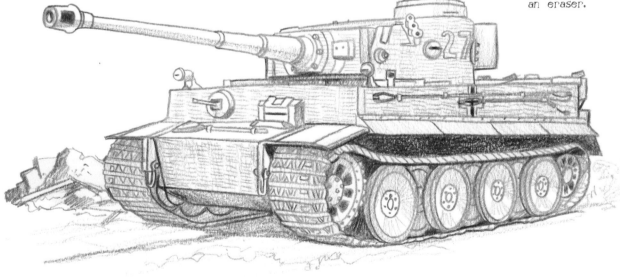

Add texture to the tracks so they look as
though they are gripping the ground.

Add shading for a three-dimensional effect. The
inner wheels, for example, receive less light than
the outer ones.

BEDFORD TRUCK

Bedford QL trucks were part of the British general supply chain during the Second World War. The QLT was the troop-carrying version.

First, sketch a large square box in perspective. It needs to be quite tall for this truck.

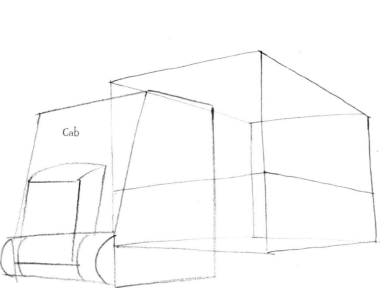

Cab

For the driver's cab, draw a smaller box with a sloping front.

Add the wheels and the curved, high wheel arch at the front.

Add details to the cab and body. Note how the windscreen opens for ventilation.

Draw a long tube to represent the rolled-up canvas tilt.

Divide the truck body into four panels. Because of perspective, the panels appear to get smaller toward the rear.

You could leave the windscreen white to show that it is reflecting the sunlight.

Add creases to the top to show that it is made of canvas.

Use hatching (parallel lines) or cross-hatching (crisscross lines) to form the dark shadows underneath the vehicle.

25

PANTHER TANK

The German Panther was one of the most effective tanks of the Second World War. Its impressive mobility and firepower made it a match for the Russian T-34.

Draw a box in perspective, and then draw a line around it near the top. This line marks the sloping upper part of the tank's hull.

Short diagonal lines create the three-dimensional shape of the hull.

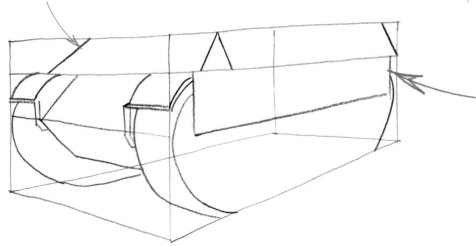

The Panther has "skirts" to protect the upper part of the caterpillar tracks. Draw these as a long rectangle on the side of the tank.

Divide the skirt into separate panels, which appear smaller toward the back.

Draw the overlapping road wheels.

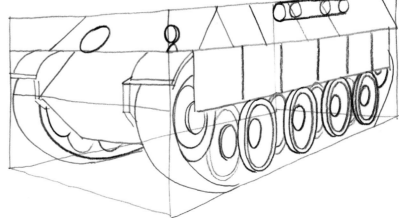

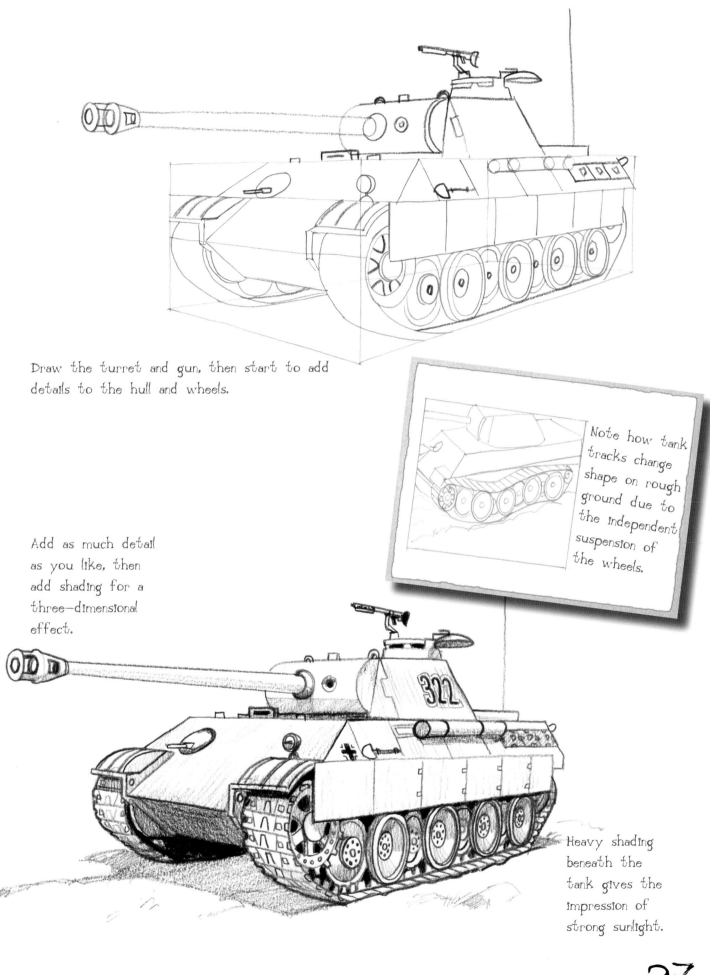

Draw the turret and gun, then start to add details to the hull and wheels.

Add as much detail as you like, then add shading for a three-dimensional effect.

Note how tank tracks change shape on rough ground due to the independent suspension of the wheels.

Heavy shading beneath the tank gives the impression of strong sunlight.

CROMWELL TANK

The British Cromwell cruiser tank was very fast and maneuverable. It was first used in northern France in June 1944. This is a Cromwell mark IV.

Outline a chunky box in perspective, with a smaller version placed on top.

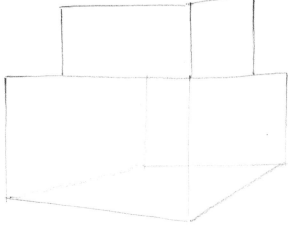

Draw the caterpillar tracks, making them narrower toward the back as they approach the vanishing point.

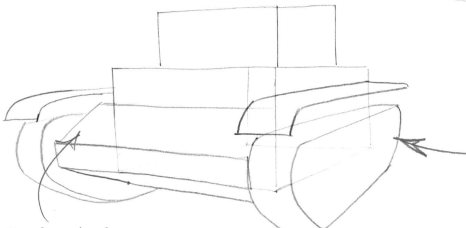

Use diagonal and horizontal lines to outline the sloping front of the hull.

Sketch in the wheels and wheel arches, and start to define the shape of the turret.

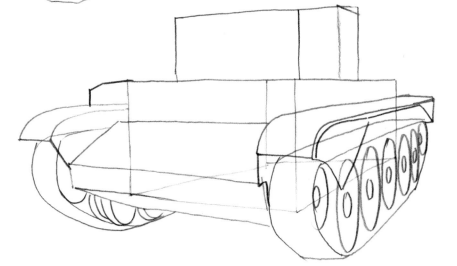

USE A MIRROR

Look at your drawing in a mirror. It's like looking at it with a fresh pair of eyes and can help you spot any mistakes.

Add as much detail as you like. The armor plating is fixed to the turret with large round bolts.

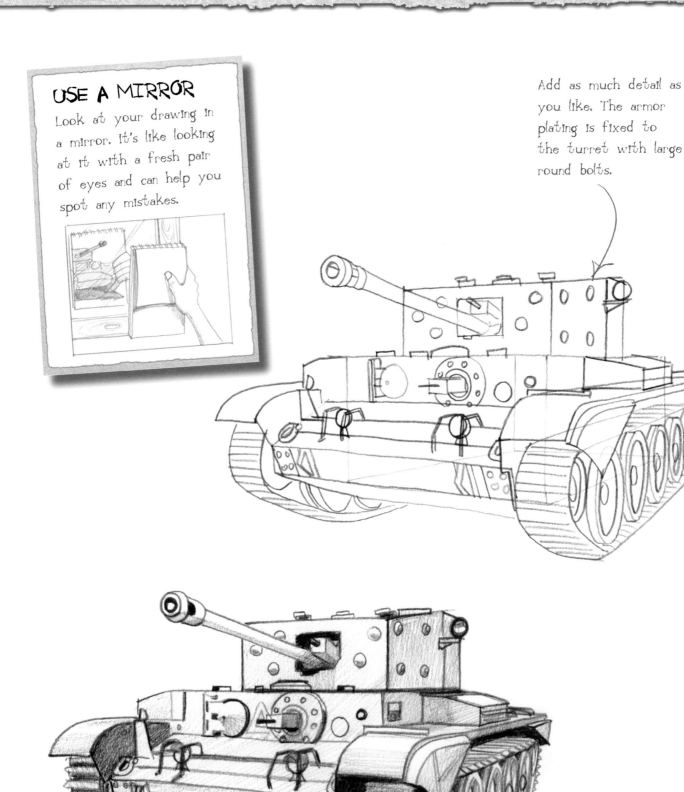

Use shading to build up the texture of the caterpillar tracks.

Shade the parts that face away from the light, such as the underside of the hull, the gun mounting, and the spaces between the wheels.

29

M1A2 ABRAMS TANK

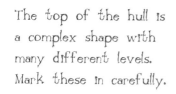

This modern American main battle tank has seen action in the Gulf War and other recent conflicts. It is protected by multiple layers of armor.

Draw a long, low box in perspective.

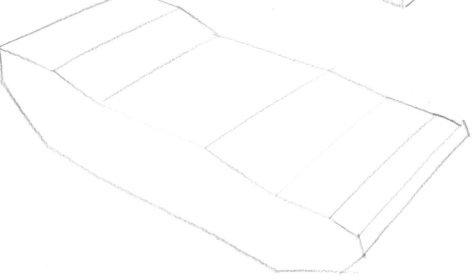

The top of the hull is a complex shape with many different levels. Mark these in carefully.

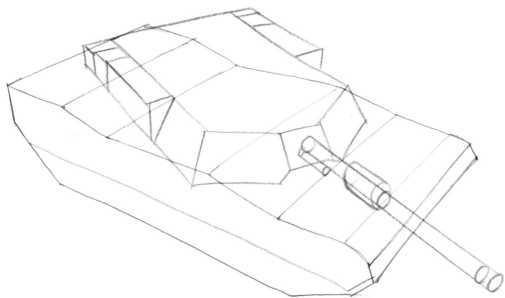

Although the turret is a complicated shape, it is composed entirely of straight lines. Turning the turret slightly to one side makes the drawing more lively.

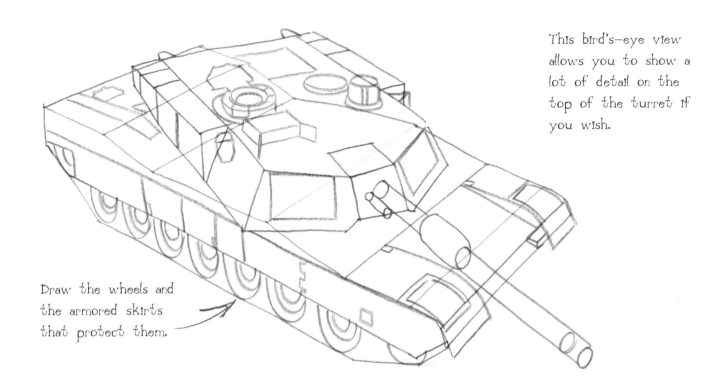

This bird's-eye view allows you to show a lot of detail on the top of the turret if you wish.

Draw the wheels and the armored skirts that protect them.

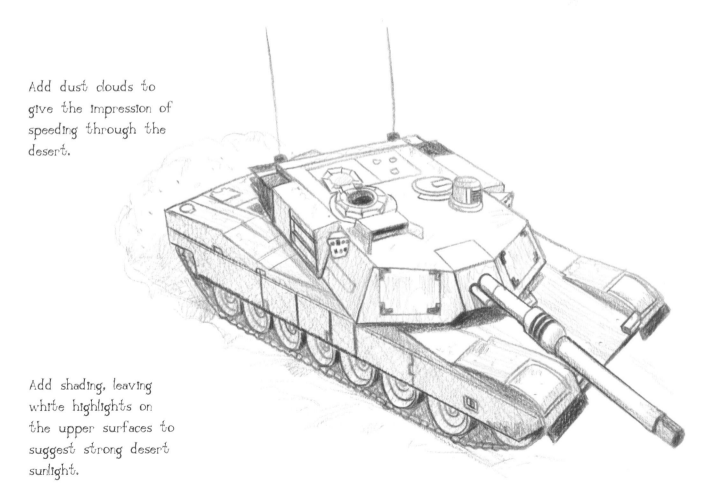

Add dust clouds to give the impression of speeding through the desert.

Add shading, leaving white highlights on the upper surfaces to suggest strong desert sunlight.

GLOSSARY

Composition The arrangement of the parts of a picture on the drawing paper.

Construction lines Guidelines used in the early stages of a drawing; they may be erased later.

Cross—hatching An area of crisscross lines used to create a dark tone.

Fixative A kind of resin sprayed over a drawing to prevent smudging. **It should only be used by an adult.**

Hatching An area of parallel lines used to create a medium tone.

Light source The direction from which the light seems to come in a drawing.

Negative space The empty spaces left between the parts of an object.

Perspective A method of drawing in which near objects are made larger than faraway objects, to suggest depth.

Proportion The correct relationship of scale between the parts of a drawing.

Silhouette A drawing that shows only a flat dark shape, like a shadow.

Tone (or shading) The use of light and dark areas in a drawing to give a three—dimensional effect.

Vanishing point (V.P.) The place in a perspective drawing where parallel lines appear to meet.

INDEX